BOARD SPORTS

Michael Hurley

Raintree

Chicago, Illinois

www.heinemannraintree.com
Visit our website to find out more information about Heinemann-Raintree books.

To order:
☎ Phone 888-454-2279
💻 Visit www.heinemannraintree.com to browse our catalog and order online.

Edited by Rebecca Rissman, Dan Nunn, and Catherine Veitch
Designed by Joanna Hinton Malivoire
Picture research by Ruth Blair
Originated by Capstone Global Library
Printed and bound in China by CTPS

15 14 13 12 11
10 9 8 7 6 5 4 3 2 1

Library of Congress Cataloging-in-Publication Data
Hurley, Michael.
  Board sports / Michael Hurley.
    p. cm.—(Extreme sports)
  Includes bibliographical references and index.
  ISBN 978-1-4109-4217-3 (hc)—ISBN 978-1-4109-4224-1 (pb) 1. Extreme sports. I. Title.
  GV749.7.H87 2012
  796.04′6—dc22   2010042357

Acknowledgments
We would like to thank the following for permission to reproduce photographs: Alamy pp. 16 (© bilwissedition Ltd. & Co. KG), 27 (© First Light); Corbis pp. 8 (© Bettmann), 11 (© Imagemore Co., Ltd.), 13 (© Bob Frid), 14 (© Drew Kelly Photography), 17 (© Stephen Frink), 19 (© Carson Ganci/Design Pics); Getty Images pp. 15 (Evan Agostini), 18 (Chris Cole), 23 (Peter Cade), 24 (Aurora/Joe McBride); Photolibrary pp. 5 (Imagestate Pictor), 7 (Superstock/Bill Stevenson), 25 (Images.com/Bonini Steve); Shutterstock pp. 4 (© ARENA Creative), 6 (© Max Earey), 9 (© Mana Photo), 10 (© EpicStock), 12 (© Maxim Petrichuk), 21 (© JOANCHANG), 20 (© Alexander Kolomietz), 22 (© EpicStock), 26 (© Igor Janicek), 28 (© takayuki), 29 (© Jaimie Duplass).

Cover photograph of a snowboarder frozen in mid-flight reproduced with permission of Corbis (© Mike Chew).

Every effort has been made to contact copyright holders of material reproduced in this book. Any omissions will be rectified in subsequent printings if notice is given to the publisher.

All the Internet addresses (URLs) given in this book were valid at the time of going to press. However, due to the dynamic nature of the Internet, some addresses may have changed, or sites may have changed or ceased to exist since publication. While the author and publisher regret any inconvenience this may cause readers, no responsibility for any such changes can be accepted by either the author or the publisher.

Some words are shown in bold, **like this**. You can find out what they mean by looking in the glossary.

Contents

What Are Board Sports?

Board sports are fun and exciting. There are many different extreme board sports, including surfing, skateboarding, and snowboarding.

Some board sports can be dangerous. To enjoy some extreme board sports, you need special **equipment** and **protective** clothing. Remember that safety is important! Look on page 26 to find some safety tips for board sports.

Surfing

Surfing became popular as a sport in the 1950s and 1960s. Surfboards were heavy and made of wood. Today, boards are made from tougher, lighter materials. They have fins at the back to help the surfer balance the board on the water.

WOW!

Kelly Slater from the United States has won the World Surfing Championships nine times.

Professional surfers ride their surfboards along massive waves. These waves can be over 33 feet high. That is taller than a two-story house!

DID YOU KNOW?
Minimals are good surfboards for beginners. Long boards and short boards are for more advanced surfers.

long board

short board

Snowboarding

Snowboarding is sometimes called surfing on snow. Your feet are attached to the board with **bindings**. Some boards are made for speed. Other boards are made for performing tricks. A snowboarder performs tricks while sliding.

WOW!

A **half-pipe** is a U-shaped track on which snowboarders can perform tricks.

Skateboarding

Skateboarding began in the 1950s. It is now one of the most popular sports in the world. You need to have good balance to be able to skateboard well.

Skateboarders are always **inventing** new, more difficult tricks and jumps. **Skate parks** have been built all over the world for skateboarders to practice on.

Kite Surfing

Kite surfing combines surfing with kite flying. Kite surfing began in China in the 1100s. Canoes were fitted with sails to catch the wind. It was called kite sailing. Kite surfing is a very physical extreme sport. It exercises your whole body.

WOW!

The time a kite surfer hangs in the air is called **hang time**. Adam Koch of the United States has a record hang time of 13 seconds!

Wakeboarding

Wakeboarding is a combination of surfing and water skiing. Your feet are strapped to a board. You ride through the **wake** caused by the boat that is pulling you along. You can use the wake to do jumps and tricks.

Windsurfing

A windsurfer is a surfboard with a sail. You hold on to a bar to control the sail. The wind blows against the sail, and that moves you through the water. People who windsurf can perform tricks, too.

WOW!

The fastest speed on a windsurfer is 54.10 knots (62 miles per hour). That is almost as fast as a cheetah can run!

Bodyboarding

Bodyboarding is a popular water sport. Athletes use boards, sometimes called "boogie boards," to do tricks in the water.

WOW!
You need shoes called **swim fins** to bodyboard properly. They help you to steer and control the board.

Mountain Boarding

In 1992 two Americans **invented** mountain boarding. They wanted to be able to practice snowboarding during the summer months, when there was no snow. Today, mountain boarders perform tricks while racing downhill.

Be Safe!

When you are taking part in board sports, it is important to be safe. You should always wear the proper **equipment**. Make sure you listen to **experts** and take many lessons.

An adult should always be with you if you are going to take part in any extreme sports.

Get Fit!

Good balance and strong legs help with board sports. Practice keeping your balance by standing on one foot for 30 seconds. Try to stay as upright as possible, and don't let your other foot touch the ground. Then repeat this on the other foot.

Try this lunge exercise to help your legs get stronger. Bend one leg in front of you. Put all your weight on the bent leg, and hold the position for 30 seconds. Straighten the leg, then try bending the other leg out in front.

Glossary

bindings fastenings that hold boots onto a snowboard

equipment tools or clothing that you need

expert person with a special skill or knowledge

half-pipe large area of snow that is cut out in the shape of the bottom half of a pipe

hang time time a kite surfer spends in the air while performing a trick

invent to be the first to think of, or make, something

professional someone who is very good at something and gets paid to do it

protective something that stops you from being harmed or injured

skate park human-made area that has been specially created for skateboarders to practice on. Skate parks include ramps and metal rails.

swim fins long plastic shoes that are shaped like webbed feet

wake track left in the water after something has moved through it

Find Out More

Books

Doeden, Matt. *To the Extreme: Snowboarding.* Mankato, Minn.: Capstone, 2005.

Mason, Paul. *Passport to World Sports: Skateboarding: The World's Coolest Skate Spots and Techniques.* Mankato, Minn.: Capstone, 2010.

Mason, Paul. *Passport to World Sports: Windsurfing: The World's Windiest Water Sport Spots and Techniques.* Mankato, Minn.: Capstone, 2010.

Websites

www.kidnetic.com
This website has lots of information about healthy eating and exercise. Why not get fit and enjoy some extreme sports?

http://kidshealth.org/kid/stay_healthy/food/sports.html
Find out more about eating well and playing sports.

www.usasa.org
This is the website of the United States of America Snowboard Association.

Index